EDINBURGH BUSES OF THE 1970s

GEORGE FAIRBAIRN

CW00550882

AMBERLEY

First published 2016

Amberley Publishing
The Hill, Stroud
Gloucestershire, GL5 4EP

www.amberley-books.com

Copyright © George Fairbairn, 2016

The right of George Fairbairn to be identified as the Author
of this work has been asserted in accordance with the
Copyrights, Designs and Patents Act 1988.

British Li brary Cataloguing in Publication Data.
A catalogue record for this book is available from the British Library.

ISBN 978 1 4456 5126 2 (print)
ISBN 978 1 4456 5127 9 (ebook)

Typeset in 10pt on 13pt Sabon.
Typesetting and Origination by Amberley Publishing.
Printed in the UK.

Introduction

The haar has blown up the Firth of Forth from the North Sea, and creeps up Granton Road from the harbour. At the bus stop outside the former Granton Road station, I can barely see the Italian tobacconist's across the road, where my granddad sends me to get his quarter ounce of ready-rubbed for his pipe. Looking down the road, all I can make out is the white blanket of the mist.

A faint sound can be heard, getting louder – the rattle of a large diesel engine. The bus is coming. Even at a tender age, I can tell even before I see the bus that this is the higher-pitched whine of the buses that usually find themselves on services 8, 14 or 19, rather than the more masculine grumble that accompanies those on the 9 or 10.

By the beginning of the 1970s I had learned enough to tell you that the whine belonged to the Gardner-engined Guy Arab IVs, with their challenging constant-mesh gearbox, and the deeper note came from the Leyland Titan PD2s, bought in large numbers for tram replacement. At that time the vast majority of the Edinburgh double-deck fleet was front-engined, and of those the vast majority were rear entrance, but by the end of the decade virtually all the deckers were one-person-operated rear-engine vehicles. At the end of the decade the government had announced the phasing out of the New Bus Grant, introduced shortly before the beginning of the '70s. The grant had discounted the purchase of new buses by up to 50 per cent. Bus lanes, limited stop services and change-free fare collection all made their appearance in Edinburgh in the 1970s.

What follows is a selection of images that I hope illustrate some of the developments of Edinburgh's municipal buses in the 1970s. I make no claim that these are in any way comprehensive; the pictures are mostly from the north and centre of the city, and reflect my interests of the time. The captions are based on my notes made at the time and information from contemporaneous sources. I have exerted myself to ensure that the information presented is accurate.

I took almost all these photographs myself. A very small number are from others who have very kindly agreed to my reproducing them, whose copyright is indicated, and to whom I am immensely grateful. I am also indebted to my wife for putting up with me chasing buses all these years, and our daughter Sarah for her invaluable advice on the text.

At the very end of their working lives at the start of the 1970s were the all-Leyland PD2/12s of 1952. They looked handsome when delivered, their exposed radiators complementing the lines of the body. In mid-life Edinburgh Corporation rebuilt them with a BMMO-style front, to harmonise their appearance with that of the other double-deckers in the fleet – though whether that was an improvement is a matter of opinion. 252 (KFS 943), recently withdrawn, awaits potential purchasers at Central garage in late 1970.

Several of the PD2/12s went for further service – some (KFS 950/51) to Hawker Siddley Aviation for use as staff transport at their Broughton plant in North Wales, and some (including JWS 652 and KFS 945/50/51) to Paton of Renfrew. A more travelled example, 242 (JFS 657) passed to the 24th Inverleith Venture Scouts, Edinburgh, who used it for four years on trips to Europe and even North Africa. The bus is seen here on the outskirts of Marrakesh. (Courtesy of Alastair Reid of the 13th Edinburgh Scouts)

I look upon the Alexander-bodied Guy Arab IVs of 1956 with fondness. They often announced their arrival before they were seen; the characteristic Gardner engine noise combined with the whine of the constant mesh transmission was unmistakeable. The rounded domes at the front and rear combined with the upstairs windows, slightly larger than those on the Orions, gave them a more airy feel. They are one of the few types of buses I have ever travelled on that had their own distinctive smell, coming in part from hot friction lining as drivers slipped the clutch to avoid the travails of wrestling too often with the unforgiving gearbox.

This image shows 935 (NSF 935) in June 1970, about to head up The Mound. At that time, the traffic at this junction was controlled by a pair of police officers on point duty who co-ordinated their efforts by subtle cues and signals. It was an art form and one which is now sadly lost. (Courtesy of Donald Hudson)

The Arab IV's favoured routes in my part of Edinburgh were the 8, 14 and 19. They could, however, be found on just about any service when the need arose. Though of the same vintage as the Orions, they were withdrawn sooner, perhaps because the fleet was standardising on the Leyland product or because the drivers found them more taxing.

NSF 934 awaits further duties at Central garage, Annandale Street. Few of these Guys were sold for further service and none are known to survive. As with King Arthur, there are tales that one example lies inactive in some remote part of Wales, awaiting the right person to call it back to life – though like that Royal archetype, no proof of its continued existence has ever been found.

A side-by-side comparison of NSF 926, an Alexander-bodied Guy Arab, and YWS 617, a later Leyland PD2A/30 with similar body, at Central garage in the early 1970s.

No discussion of Edinburgh's buses in the 1970s, or in the preceding two decades, can ignore the immense influence of the 300 MCW-bodied Leyland Titan PD2/20s purchased as part of the tram replacement program and delivered between 1954 and 1957.

Leyland Titan PD2/20, with MCW bodywork, 500 (LFS 500) at Pilrig in 1975. The bus shows the rather broad, thin numerals still to be found in the 1970s on buses fitted with older blinds.

715 (NSF 715), one of the 1956 delivery of PD2/20s, passes the end of Boswall Green on its way to Granton Square. The winter sun's low light shows up the angular treatment of the cab sides. They were famously and unfavourably described in the Edinburgh council chambers by Baillie A. J. Cabas, 'They are ungainly, inelegant, monstrous masses of shivering tin. They are modern to the extent of being able to produce a perfect synchronisation of rock and roll.'

Leyland Titan PD2/20 497 (LFS 497), with MCW bodywork, speeds up Frederick Street with a good downstairs load and a solitary smoker on the upper deck. The bus was withdrawn in April 1975.

LFS 482 ascends Granton Road on service 9. It is still fitted with the earlier style of grille, with only four shorter central slots. Later vehicles had eight shorter slots in the centre with two longer slots on each side. 482 was withdrawn at the end of 1975 and was scrapped in Barnsley early the next year.

LWS 519 begins the climb from Bellevue up Broughton Road to Picardy Place on service 9 in the summer of 1975. It was withdrawn at the end of that year and subsequently scrapped.

587 (LWS 587) heads through West Port, shortly before withdrawal in 1975.

As originally conceived, the Orions had no vents in any of the side windows. Even Edinburgh, though, can get a little warm at times, and this omission was fairly quickly rectified. There were minor differences between examples, but for the large part these buses were all identical and lived lengthy and productive lives pounding the streets of Edinburgh and, in turn, being pounded by the cobbles.

Edinburgh Corporation Leyland Titan PD2/20 542 (LWS 542), with MCW bodywork, leaves Edinburgh's historic Grassmarket and heads up Candlemaker Row on service 2 in late 1973.

A typical scene of service 23 at the Trinity terminus on Lennox Row in the early 1970s, Leyland Titan PD2/20 573 (LWS 573) disgorging its passengers. The conductor leans nonchalantly on the side of his bus; he and the driver will shortly spend a few minutes in conversation and perhaps each light up a cigarette before the return journey to Morningside.

Service 23 still uses this terminus today, over forty years later, having migrated here from Granton Road station on the closure of the tramway system in 1956. 523 was withdrawn at the end of 1975 and scrapped in 1976.

After they were displaced by driver-only operated Atlanteans, as they had in their time displaced the trams, many Orions went for scrap. Despite their advancing years, numbers of them were sold for further service in Tayside and in South Wales, and as factory transport for workers at Lesney's plant in London, where Matchbox model cars and buses were made. Some were converted into playbuses and some as trainers. Over sixty years after they first arrived in Edinburgh, examples remain in preservation.

Seen here is a line-up of PD2 Orions at Marine garage. At the head is former 778, OFS 778, a 1957 bus. After withdrawal it was converted into a playbus for East Lothian social services. Similar buses converted at the same time were OFS 794 and 795.

Leyland Titan PD2/20 OFS 799, bodied by MCW, had a long and varied life in Edinburgh. New in November 1957, it provided passenger service until the latter half on 1974 when it was withdrawn and converted into trainer T14. It retained this role till the summer of 1976 when it was repainted, as seen here, to promote and sell the Ridacard range of season passes that were introduced on 4 July 1976. Following that campaign it was unused for some time before being reinstated as trainer TB14, still in the all-yellow scheme, in May of 1979, by which time it was well into its twenty-second year.

After the resolute functionality of the Orions, Edinburgh's next double-decked purchases were of an altogether more flamboyant style. PWS 998 and 999 were Alexander-bodied Titan PD3/2s. 998, photographed turning into Granton Road in 1972, was famously equipped with a Homalloy front, blue upholstery and automatic transmission. 999 featured a cherry-red livery. A subsequent batch of 4 PD3/3s, SWS 261–64, came in 1959. Their usual stamping ground was service 19 and all were sold to Highland Omnibuses in 1974.

After the flirtation with longer buses, Edinburgh returned to the PD2 series for the 1960 deliveries. These were to be the last rear-loaders purchased by the city.

628 (YWS 628) heads eastwards along Starbank Road at Newhaven in 1976. Granton Harbour is visible in the background. The Alexander-bodied Leyland Titan PD2A/30 was withdrawn that same year and sold to South Wales Training Centre, Swansea, where it was employed as a driver trainer.

In 1966 Edinburgh Corporation committed itself to 30-foot deckers with the purchase of fifty PD3/6s. By this time Leyland were fitting the concealed-radiator version of the Titan with the more sculptural St Helen's front, but Edinburgh insisted on specifying their traditional slatted grille, variously known as a tin or BMMO front. It was in this form that the Alexander-bodied vehicles 651–700 (ASC 651–700B) arrived.

677 (ASC 677B) is parked on Lauriston Place outside George Heriot's School in 1977. This regular hire transported students from the school to the playing fields at Goldenacre, some 2½ miles to the north.

Just a few weeks before Lothian Region Transport came into being, ECT 666 (ASC 666B), a Leyland Titan PD3/6 with Alexander body, waits to turn left out of Forest Road and head towards the Grassmarket on service 2. An Austin FX4 taxi waits beside it and in the distance a Shelvoke & Drewry waste collection lorry goes about its business. 666 was sold in the summer of 1977 to Moffat, Cardenden, but the following year returned to the capital in the ownership of Curran, Edinburgh.

A 1975 view of a scene much changed since by later development finds a 1964 Leyland Titan PD3/6, bodied by Alexander, at the terminus of service 9 outside HMS Claverhouse, the then training centre of the Forth Division, Royal Naval Reserve. Parallel to and on the far side of Lower Granton Road, behind the bus, were the tracks of the Edinburgh, Perth & Dundee Railway.

Saturday 6 December 1975, the last day of crew operation on services 9 and 10, found Leyland Titan PD3/6 660 (ASC 660B) on Granton Road with the damp streets and low sun making life difficult for the photographer. 660 was later sold to Rapson's, Brora.

Leaving Granton and passing along Lower Granton Road, Leyland Titan PD3/6 658 (ASC 658B) heads towards Newhaven with the railway, which at the time was still open for traffic to Granton Harbour, on the right.

The Alexander-bodied bus was loaned to Scottish Omnibuses in July 1977 and was still there in September. However, an industrial dispute at Lothian Region adversley affected vehicle availablilty and 658 was reclaimed to cover for defective buses. 658 was one of the last PD3/6s in service, remaining active after newer vehicles had been withdrawn on expiry of their Certificates of Fitness.

Numerically the last of the PD3/6s, Alexander-bodied Leyland Titan 700 (ASC 700B) loads at the foot of The Mound. It was withdrawn in November 1976 and purchased by Maclennan, Spitalfield.

Edinburgh's final intake of front-engined double-deckers were 826–50 (EWS 826–50D) of 1966. These were Leyland Titan PD3A/2s. As with the preceeding PD3/6s, Leyland no longer supplied chassis with the bonnet and grille that Edinburgh specified. These last examples left the Lancashire factory as exposed-radiator vehicles and were subsequently modified before entering service with Alexander bodies and BMMO-style grilles. They were unique in Edinburgh in having rotavent ventilators and had rather attractive full-colour badges featuring the Edinburgh crest fitted above the grille, where previously a simplified white-on-black castle motif had been used. They were regular performers on service 1, replacing Tiger Cubs once various bridge clearance problems had been resolved, but here 829 is on service 19 as it stops at Wardie to pick up passengers.

For about a year from December 1975, 829 wore a broadside advertisement for Sony Hi-Fi audio systems.

As the last manual gearbox vehicles were leaving the fleet the requirements for trainers changed and semi-automatic buses were drafted. 829 became TB7 in late 1978 and is seen here awaiting further trainees at Marine garage.

Crew changeovers from Central garage for some services could conveniently take place at Bellevue, opposite East Claremont Street. A number of crew members take in the sun while a driver boards Titan 828 (EWS 828D) at the start of his shift.

This 1977 view finds 835 (EWS 835D) in Davidson's Mains. This bus had the distinction of being the last of Lothian's PD3A/2s to be withdrawn, in July 1979, and was then sold to Pettigrew, Mauchline.

The last of the Titans was delivered in September 1966, and they were immediately followed by Edinburgh's first volume purchase of Atlantean PDR1/1s. The very first Atlantean for Edinburgh, 801 (ESF 801C), had arrived in February 1966.

When new, Alexander-bodied Atlantean PDR1/1 802 (EWS 802D) went to Edinburgh's Italian twin town Florence, and acquired a GB plate that it continued proudly to display for the rest of its career. By the time of this 1975 photograph outside Marine garage, it had become a little faded but was still clearly visible. Also, note the advertisement for the well-known motor dealer Moir & Baxter, and the now long-vanished marques available from them.

Edinburgh's only short-windowed Atlanteans were 803–25 (EWS 803–35), delivered in 1966 in tandem with its last front-engined double-deckers, EWS 826–50. In OMO condition and fitted with Autofare, 819 loads outside the Scotch House on Princes Street in 1975. The similar 812 is preserved.

This bus was sold to Key Coachways, Rugely, in 1983.

One of the twenty-five Leyland Atlantean PDR1/1s of 1966, 821 (EWS 821D) is seen here at Surgeon's Hall in 1977. In this year, the stickers on either side of the destination display, advising passengers of the Autofare system on the bus, were judged redundant and removed. A ghost of their presence remains visible on the bus as the slightly darker shade of madder on the areas they had covered.

A rear three-quarter view of Atlantean PDR1/1 824 (EWS 824D) as it heads up Stirling Road, Trinity, shows the shrouds specified by Edinburgh on its Atlanteans to disguise the appearance of the engine 'bustle' on its early rear-engined double-deckers.

The 1968 deckers were all Alexander-bodied Atlanteans, a choice that was to continue till the Olympian replaced its venerable predecessor in the 1980s. 859 (JSC 859E), a Leyland Atlantean PDR1/1 with Alexander body, awaits its next duty at Central garage in 1975.

The West Approach Road, built on the alignment of former railway lines leading to Princes Street station, opened in 1975 and Edinburgh Corporation provided bus tours of the new facility at the time. 923 (OSF 923M) and 851 (JSC 851E) did the honours, and the latter is seen here passing under Gardner's Crescent. The section of the route visible behind the bus has since changed beyond all recognition.

Edinburgh Corporation 900 (JSC900E) of 1968, seen outside STV's Gateway Studios on Leith Walk. This was the first example of the PDR2/1 model built to the new maximum length of 33 feet to enter service; its Alexander H47/35F body was distinguishable from the other Atlaneans by the little window at the back of the top deck. The sliding vents were added later in life when operating experience revealed that the ventilation system of the panoramic-windowed buses was not as effective as had been hoped.

A rare interior view of the upper deck of 900 in its closed-top form. 900 remained the only Atlantean of this length in the Edinburgh and Lothian fleets. It was later converted to open-top and is now preserved in that form.

Numerically the first of Edinburgh's dual-door double-deckers was 301 (PSC 301G), a 1969 Leyland Atlantean PDR1A/1 with Alexander B45/39D body. In this 1973 image it is on one of the early OMO routes, service 8, about to turn right into Inverleith Row from Ferry Road, with the tower on Inverleith church visible in the background.

On 30 March 1972, Edinburgh Corporation Transport introduced service 43, Waverley–Wester Hailes. Alexander-bodied 1969 Leyland Atlantean 313 (PSC 313G) waits at the departure point on Waverley Bridge the following year. This service and service 30 were the first to be converted to Autofare.

The photo shows that its front panel has been replaced, presumably as a result of accident damage, by one of the later pattern.

Edinburgh's first new deckers of the seventies were a batch of fifty Leyland Atlantean PDR1A/1s with Alexander H45/30D bodies, substantively identical to the preceding PSC 301–50G vehicles, but with the revised front panel. Many of these were delivered in time to serve as athletes' transport for the ninth Commonwealth Games, held 17–25 July 1970. In addition, fourteen of the buses had their lower deck seats removed and were converted to take wheelchairs for the British Commonwealth Paraplegic Games that immediately followed.

After the excitement of the Games had ended, these buses entered service on more routine duties. 359 (SSF 359H) is seen on George Street on service 41, heading towards City Hospital at Greenbank, whither the route had been extended in August 1970. The lower deck window behind the staircase has acquired a sliding vent, fitted to this batch and the PSC-G buses in spring and summer 1971. The subsequent delivery of PDR1A/1 had them from new.

A queue of buses on Princes Street shows a fleet profile typical of the early to mid-1970s. AN68 905 leads the procession, followed by two PD2/20s, a PD3 and a PDR1A/1. A Tiger Cub skulks in the background.

Edinburgh's tall buldings and a low winter sun often conspire to make life difficult for the bus photographer, but can produce attractive effects, as seen here on Home Street. The spire of the Barclay Viewforth church is sillhouetted behind Alexander-bodied Lothian Region Transport Leyland Atlantean PDR1A/1 356 (SSF 356H). The last of this batch was not completed until September 1970, but managed to retain their 'H' suffix registrations, a trick that in later years would not prove possible.

1971's Atlantean intake, WFS 251–300K, started to arrive in November of that year. 269–266, from closest to camera to furthest away, await delivery at Alexander's works. These buses entered service in December of 1971, displacing Guy Arab IVs and also requiring the renumbering of Leyland Titan PD3/2s 261–4 (SWS 261–4), which became 994–7.

WFS 272K had an unusual fate: in 1989 it was one of ten buses converted into playbuses for the National Playbus Association as part of the first episode of the television programme *Challenge Anneka*. Subsequent to that it passed to the Govan Initiative Limited. (Courtesy of Barry Santana)

Two PDR1A/1s meet at Newahven. 377 (SSF 377H) faces the Forth and Fife beyond, while 275 (WFS 275K) is pointing up Craighall Road. These Alexander-bodied Atlanteans not only served together in Edinburgh, but were both subsequently acquired by Ulsterbus: 377 in December 1985 and 275 in the following January. 377 was withdrawn by Ulsterbus in June 1989 and subsequently scrapped. 275 passed to Stadium Youth and Community Centre in May 1992 and to Coleraine & District Motor Cycle Club in August 2001, where it was used as a club room for several years.

Alexander-bodied Leyland Atlantean PDR1A/1 294 (WFS 294K) passes some distinctive housing in Muirhouse on the newly enlarged service 32 in 1975. Beginning as a service between Corstorphine and Wester Hailes, by 13 April 1975 the 32 had become a lengthy circular service linking Edinburgh's outer suburbs.

A diversion in 1975 saw services operating on the Royal Mile that never normally cast shadows on that fine thoroughfare. Working a service 7, Atlantean PDR1A/1 280 (WFS 280K) descends towards Holyrood, passing the Tolbooth with an AN68 and a PDR1 in pursuit. 280 was later owned by Ulsterbus as their 900 based in Coleraine, and subsequently passed to Autograss Racing Nothern Ireland.

A classic view of Edinburgh. At the far end of North Bridge is Robert Adam's Register House with its splendid dome; to its right, the general post office. To the right of the buses, Patrick Thompson's department store, known as 'PT's' to generations of Edinburgh shoppers. Leyland Titan PD2/20 435 (LFS 435) and Leyland Atlantean 252 (WFS 252K) wait their turn at the traffic lights at the junction of North Bridge, South Bridge and the high street. 435 was offfered for sale in late summer 1974. 252 saw subsequent service after dergulation with the reconstiuted North Western, numbered 481.

An unidentified PDR1A/1 is parked at the Greenbak terminus of service 41 at Christmas 1979, just before departing on its return trip to Barnton.

The 1972 Atlanteans were a break with the past, being of the new AN68 type with revised Alexander bodywork to match. BFS 2L was shown off to the public at an open day at Shrubhill before entering service. BFS 1L, affectionately known as 'Basil', remains in preservation.

In this picture, BFS 11L heads west along West Granton Road past deck-access flats of an unusual aspect.

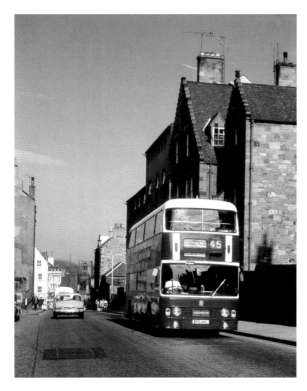

Another of the 1972 deliveries, BFS 49L ascends the Royal Mile. After its service in Edinburgh, this bus was redeployed in open-top form to Lothian's Classic Tour operation in Oxford.

Once again at Newhaven, we find Alexander-bodied Leyland Atlantean AN68 35 (BFS 35L) on Starbank Road at the foot of Craighall Road, with the iconic gasholders of Granton Gasworks in the background.

Leyland Atlantean 356 (SSF 356H) in full Setrite OMO condition lays over at the summer terminus of service 8 at Silverknowes promenade. In the winter months this service terminated at the top of this road, near the clubhouse for the adjacent municipal golf links.

This and next page: A puncture affecting the front offside wheel of AN68 48 (BFS 48L), just by Haymarket station, provided an opportunity to see how such things were dealt with in 1979. Fitters roll up in a van, or possibly another bus if more convenient. Application of a wheelbrace with a generously proportioned bar, to provide leverage, and a bottle jack enable the defective tyre and wheel to be removed while an associate rolls up the replacement. The new wheel fitted, the bus is let down from the jack and our hero dives under the front axle to remove it, while the bus driver takes a quick last draw on his cigarette. Finally, once the wheel nut guard ring is secured, the bus is ready to move.

Late 1973 saw the arrival of the first of the next batch of Leyland Atlantean AN68s. As usual, they had Alexander H45/30D bodies. 901–2 (OFS 901–2M) were fitted with CAV four-speed automatic transmission.

In 1977, 901 turns from Princes Street into The Mound on service 23, wearing an all-over advertisement for the short-lived home furnishings shop Big J Homecare. One can also see that these buses were fitted with a three-point intermediate screen – for some years prior to that, a six-point screen had been standard, though many older buses had continued to operate with the two-point screens they had been delivered with.

Alexander-bodied Leyland Atlantean AN68 903 (OFS 903M) executes the right turn from Inverleith Row into Ferry Road on service 23.

Edinburgh's first driver-only operated double-deck buses (universally described at the time as 'One Man Operated', or OMO) carried a three-spot sticker on the front tweendecks to alert intending passengers to have their fares ready. These symbols are seen here on 939 (OSF 939M) proceeding along a wet and scaffold-shrouded George Street in 1975.

Leyland Atlantean AN68 942 (OSF 942M) entered service in June 1974. It was fitted with a five-speed automatic gearbox and a SCG G2 control unit for comparison with the CAV four-speed automatic transmission on the otherwise similar 901 and 902. The outcome of the experiment was the adopton of the G2 unit for subsequent AN68 deliveries.

942 is seen here at Tollcross in 1977, with Goldberg's store just visible in the background.

One usually associates Edinburgh buses with urban surroundings, but here an unidentified AN68 on service 32 finds itself in an arboreal setting as it crosses the Water of Leith on Bridge Road near Colinton.

Freshly delivered and gleaming, Leyland Atlantean AN68 949 (OSF 949M) stands at Shrubhill works prior to entering service. The brackets for the Setright Speed ticket machine and the change hopper can be clearly seen on the side of the driver's cab. This bus, like several others of the batch, benefitted from a five-speed gearbox from new. It also had the distinction of running for a short time with an incorrect registration on the back – a plate was made up and fitted bearng the mark OFS 949M – an understandable error, as the first eighteen vehicles in this batch were registered OFS xxxM.

Travelling Edinburgh's streets can be thirsty work for buses. AN68 27 (BFS 27L) gets a top up of water from the Shell garage at the junction of Granton Road and Inverleith Row.

Summer 1976 finds Alexander-bodied Leyland Atlantean AN68 417 (GFS 417N) at the then-remote Glimerton terminus of service 8. The GFS xxxN buses omitted the illuminated 'Pay on Entry' sign beneath the number screen that had featured on the front of new deckers from the PSC xxxG batch onward, and which had been retrofitted to older Atlanteans when they were converted to driver-only operation. The ubiquity of one-person-operated buses was deemed to render this accessory redundant, although they were not removed from the earlier vehicles. In 1977, 417 was one of several Atlanteans fitted with 'Sounds in Motion', which played music on the top deck, interspersed with advertisements.

Roadworks leading to the closure of Granton Road in 1978 resulted in the diversion of buses' services onto the adjacent Wardie Road, normally unserved. A smartly dressed contingent take advantage of the opportunity and board 421 (GFS 421N), a 1974 Leyland Atlantean AN68/Alexander. The bus is stopped just beyond the bridge over the former Caledonian Railway line through Edinburgh's northern suburbs. The line closed to passengers in 1962; it has since become a cycle route.

Local government reorganisation saw the creation of Lothian Region Transport on 16 May 1975. The new organisation inherited a fleet of 681 buses: 598 deckers and 83 saloons. The former Edinburgh Corporation crest, seen above right, was rapidly subsumed by stickers carrying the coat of arms of the new authority, as seen in the lower image, together with the new legal lettering.

Titan PD2/20s 499 and 482 showing Edinburgh and Lothian crests at the open-air parking at the side of Central garage in 1975. 499 was withdrawn soon after and sold to D Coaches of Swansea, an operator who accumulated large numbers of former Edinburgh PD2s and PD3s. D Coaches operated 499 in full Edinburgh livery, complete with an advertisement for *The Scotsman* newspaper on the side, though it is not recorded if this boosted sales of the journal in South Wales.

Numerically, the last bus delivered new to Edinburgh Corporation was 450 (GFS 450N). It was still virtually new in this photograph, taken at Shrubhill works, but it had already acquired the new crest. This vehicle followed in the noble tradition of many of its Edinburgh predecessors in being loaned to other operators, in this case it was one of three AN68s that were temporarily swapped with a similar number of Nottingham Leopards in 1984/85 as, for a short time, Lothian had insufficient saloons to cover single-deck requirements.

Lothian Region Transport's first new buses were the JSG-N registered Atlanteans starting with 451, delivered in May 1975. Here is 451 (JSG 451N) heading west along Princes Street. Service 33 had been extended to Wester Hailes on June 20 1972.

Looking very shiny, 461 (JSG 461N) awaits one of its first duties at Central garage in June 1975. From early 1974, the Autofare ticketing system was introduced in Edinburgh. Autofare-equipped buses were distinguished by a white banner on each side of the front tweendecks bearing a blue stylised image representing a coin dropping into a hopper. This distinguished them from the earlier Setright-equipped vehicles, where the banners had three black dots bearing the words PAY ON ENTRY in white.

Leyland Atlantean AN68 471 (MSF 471P), with Alexander bodywork, pauses on George Street at a stop graced by one of Edinburgh's traditional bus shelters.

Lothian 490 (MSF 490P) passes St Andrew's House, at the time occupied by the Scottish Office, with the distinctive profiles of Salisbury Crags and Arthur's Seat as the backdrop. Unseen to the left is the old Royal High School.

November 1976 saw the arrival of 531 (SSG 531R), another of the many Leyland Atlantean AN68A/1Rs purchased by Lothian. Here it passes through Davidson's Mains on its way from Cramond. The SSG-R batch delivery was spread over a lengthy period, with SSG 501R arriving in August 1976 and SSG 560R in August of the next year.

568 (YSF 568S) was a Leyland Atlantean with Alexander body. New in February 1978, it is seen later that year heading east along Ferry Road clad in a broadside advertisement for American Express Travel Services.

The 1979 Atlanteans had many obvious differences from their predecessors. The destination display was revised, with all the blinds together behind a large glass panel. With an eye to the future, the twin-track front number display was replaced with a three-track unit. The passengers benefitted from the addition of new heating equipment placed under the stairs and several large hopper vents. The single-piece front windscreen was replaced with a heated, vertically split screen, and the cab layout was revised.

580 (JSX 580T) turns into Ferry Road shortly after delivery in January 1979.

One of the last deckers delivered to Lothian in the 1970s, OSC 606V is seen here upon its return from service at Marine garage. The JSX-T batch ended at 598 and the OSC-V batch picked up at 601. Fleet numbers 599 and 600 had been reserved for two Leyland Titan TN15s that Lothian had ordered and were initially expected in 1978/79 but, as a result of Leyland's closure of the Park Royal Vehicles plant, were never built. 606 was new in August 1979.

Edinburgh Corporation 101 (YSG 101) was an early Alexander Y-type bodied Leyland Leopard which, when new, had a then unique (for the UK) three-door layout, thus predating the three-door London 'Borismaster' LT class by some fifty years. Later, in the 1960s, it was converted to a more conventional single-door layout and used as an Airport Express coach with conventional bus seats. In this guise I found it at Central garage, in the company of Duple-bodied Bedford SB5 221 (221 FS).

Changing requirements led to a third phase in the career of 101. Demoted from airport coach in 1975, it once again donned madder and white, this time in single-doorway format, and was fitted with Autofare for service 49 as a bus. This photograph captures it at the Marine garage open day in 1979, with a somewhat imaginative destination display. It retained this front-entrance layout till withdrawal, but has since been preserved in its original three-door format.

The mainstay of saloon bus operations in Edinburgh for the early part of the 1970s were fifty Weymann-bodied Leyland Tiger Cubs, part of a large number new in 1959 and 1960. A 1975 view shows Leyland Tiger Cub 80 (VSC 80) on Sleigh Drive at Lochend. It is about to depart on service 13 to the West End.

Another view of 80, with a vista behind stretching all the way down the Leith and the Forth, and the green slopes of Calton Hill on the right. All this is now obscured by buildings. The change hopper is also clearly visible. Non-Autofare driver-operated Tiger Cubs did not carry the 'Pay on Entry' stickers that appeared on similarly equipped double-deckers.

Limited Stop service 75 was converted from double- to single-deck operation on 28 October 1974, and shortly after that date I found Weymann-bodied Leyland Tiger Cub PSUC1/3 63 (VSC 63) heading towards the city centre on York Place. 63 had been converted to driver-only operation in August 1972, while Service 75 was withdrawn 24 May 1976 and replaced with a new limited stop service 86. 63 was sold to Holmeswood Coaches in early 1977.

Leyland Tiger Cub 78 (VSC 78) collects a member of staff from the stop conveniently placed near Central garage. 78 was converted to driver-only Autofare operation in October 1974.

Descending the high street, Weymann-bodied Leyland Tiger Cub PSUC1/3 58 (VSC 58) looks the worse for wear, especially in the windscreen wiper department. The bus had been converted to Autofare in October 1976, shortly before I took this photograph. St Giles' Cathedral dominates the background. Service 60 was previously worked by Seddon Midis but operating experience led to them being replaced by Tiger Cubs from 6 January 1974.

Tiger Cub 76 (VSC 76) looking a little tired towards the end of its life, at Marine garage.

86 (VSC 86) returns to Marine garage at the end of its final shift before withdrawal. The bus was purchased for preservation.

The first half of 1973 saw the arrival of ten Seddon Pennine Midibuses, 102–11 (BWS 102–5L, CFS 106–11L). They had a chequered history as they were not popular with drivers, and by the end of 1974 were usually only to be found on service 61, a hail-a-bus route serving Ravelston. 108 was loaned to Merseyside in 1974 and to Tayside on September 1976, with Tayside eventually buying some former Greater Manchester PTE examples.

Seen here is BWS 105L awaiting custom at Turnhouse Airport on service 25. This bus is now preserved.

One of the less usual duties of Edinburgh buses at the time was to assist in the collection of ballot papers from polling places at elections. Here, 102 (BFS 102L) is boarded by a police officer carrying election-related materials at Wardie Primary School in 1974.

By November 1974, the Seddons were usually only to be found on service 61. This operated as a hail-a-bus service in the outer part of its route in Ravelstone Dykes, where it had a meandering route through the streets and passengers could be picked up and set down at any suitable point rather than at defined bus stops. The service was discontinued on 29 May 1977.

Seen here, 107 (CFS 107L) waits on Frederick Street at the city centre end of the service.

A small number of Ford Transits were operated from Marine garage. 150 (SFS 150R) is typical. It was a diesel-engined vehicle with bodywork by Solent. The Transits were not used on PSV duties but as crew shuttle and for other similar tasks. After service with Lothian, the bus passed to Garret Coach Hire of Tonbridge.

One of the more unusual vehicles operated by Lothian Region Transport was 146 (TSY 968M). This Dormobile-bodied petrol-engined Bedford CFL was purchased by Midlothian County Council and inherited by Lothian Region Transport in the local council reorganisation of May 1975. It was based at Marine but operated a minibus service in Currie on the other side of the city.

The Ratho service evolved into the Newbridge Intervillage Service visiting Currie, Hermiston, Dalmahoy, Ratho and Newbridge, and running Mondays to Thursdays only. Here, little Seddon 103 (BWS 103L) heaves itself across the bridge over the Union Canal in Ratho in 1979.

At the beginning of the 1970s, Edinburgh's coach fleet included this 1964 Duple-bodied Bedford VAS, 222 (222 FS). In 1976 it was reseated as a bus and repainted madder and white, a fate that had befallen the similar 201–3SC a year earlier.

Fords were never a prominent part of the Edinburgh or Lothian fleet. One of the few full-sized Ford PSVs operated was 227 (MSF 227F), a 1968 R226 with Duple (Northern) C52F body. By the time of this photograph in 1975 it was delicensed and parked up in Central garage awaiting disposal.

Another coach at least nominally part of the Edinburgh fleet as the seventies commenced was 123, formerly 822 (PSW 822). This was the corporation's only Albion Aberdonian and had Alexander bodywork. Originally a bus, its career followed a trajectory opposite to that of the Bedford VASs in that it was converted to a coach, but it spent a lot of its time immobile at the rear of Central garage, where I photographed it in the company of LFS 500, numerically the last of the 1954 intake of PD2/20s for tram replacement. 123 appears to be in a neglected and part-cannibalised state. 500 was sold to D Coaches, Morriston, Swansea, who operated it for several years.

The Bedford/Duple combination was typical of Edinburgh's coach fleet in the first half of the seventies. An example is 231 (PSC 231G), a 1969 vintage Bedford VAM70 with Duple Viceroy bodywork. It was photographed in 1971 in Central garage.

The 1970 intake of coaches included SSF 237H, a Bedford VAL70 with Duple Viceroy bodywork. Withdrawn in 1978, the coach passed to Brown of Builth Wells and, after being in their ownership for many years, was acquired for preservation and now resides at the Scottish Vintage Bus Museum.

The 1972 coach deliveries were outwardly very similar to their predecessors. However, they included some of the first examples of Bedford's new YRT chassis. These received some of the last examples of Duple's Viceroy body, and were thus a most unusual combination. AFS 245K enters St Andrew Square while its sister 247 takes on a load for the then-new Asda store to the north-west of the city. 245 was written off after an accident in 1981.

Edinburgh's adherence to the Bedford/Duple combination for its coaching fleet continued with the arrival of the latter's Dominant model, supplied on Bedford YRT chassis as seen here on 206 (NFS 206M), new in August 1973. Although intended for coach work such as tours and private hires, in a highly unusual move 206 has been pressed into stage carriage service on service 9 and is seen on the outer extremeties of the service approaching the terminus at Torphin in the summer of 1975.

Later in its life, 206 could readily be distinguished from the otherwise similar vehicles in the fleet by the white panel surrounding the grille and headlights: Edinburgh usually painted this component black. It is parked here on the Castle Esplanade in the shadow of the spectator seating being assembled for the 1979 Edinburgh Military Tattoo. Beside it sits its 1976 equivalent, 226 (PSF 226P), a Bedford YMT with similar Duple bodywork. A passing young man displays the fashions of the day.

The 1975 coach requirement was, in contrast, supplied by Alexander Y-type bodied Bedford YRTs. In its first year of operation, 116 (GSX 116N) pauses outside Canongate Kirk. Note the driver in his Tours uniform, and the Autofare hopper, black instead of the usual red to fit in with the restrained image of the coach fleet.

In the summer of 1976, 117 (GSX 117N), newly relettered with Lothian fleet names, descends Leith Walk. This vehicle later passed to Minsterley Motors, Shropshire, who operated it in Edinburgh madder and white.

In 1976, the 1975 Bedfords were repainted from black and white to madder and white and found themselves on bus services, though initially at least they retained their coach-style seating. 119 (GSX 119N) is seen in 1976 heading towards Turnhouse Airport.

112–15 had slightly different destination equipment from the rest of the batch. Like the Seddon Midis, they had two-aperture boxes, as seen here on 115 (GSX 115N) operating a school service with a somewhat unruly collection of passengers. It is ascending Granton Road – Granton Harbour is visible in the background. Between 1850 and the opening of the Forth Bridge in 1890, the ferry carrying coaches and wagons of the Edinburgh & Northern Railway departed from the ramp visible just to the left of the large shed with the white gable end, sloping down to the right and into the water. The street lamp is mounted on a traction pole from the former tramway system, which had closed over twenty years previously.

In February 1977, 115, together with sister vehicle 117, was repainted in a dedicated livery for service 38. The idea of an eyecatching livery to promote the service, revolutionary in Edinburgh at the time, was promulgated by a local councillor. A large number 38 on the side, accompanied by the slogan 'Your Local Bus' and a list of intermediate places served displayed above the cantrail, completed the effect and by the summer of that year the service had seen a 30 per cent increase in traffic.

Operating experience with the Y-type YRTs and Leopards led to the decision to swap the seating, as the heavyweight Leopards were better suited to lengthy private hires than the medium-weight Bedfords. 116 (GSX 116N) circumnavigates Drummond Place with its newly installed bus seating clearly in view.

1976 saw a reversion to the Bedford/Duple combination, though the chassis had evolved to the YNT model by this time. 223 (PSF 223P) heels over hard as it turns right from Waverley Bridge into Princes Street with a good load on a Winter's City Tour.

PSF 223P again, outside Holyrood Palace, waits the return of its passengers from a tour of the historic building.

Lothian Region Transport converted some of the 1968 batch of Atlanteans to somewhat coachlike appearance for the 1976 city tours. The second vehicle modifed, 860 (JSC 860E), stands on Waverly Bridge in summer 1976, about to depart on 'The Sea The City and The Hills' tour. As can just be seen, the seating retained the same frames, but the red upholstery was replaced by a yellow tartan material rather unflatteringly dubbed 'McTartan'. The double-deck tours proved so popular that later that year they were extended through the winter season at weekends.

The 1978 coach deliveries showed a complete change of direction. 230 (EFS 230S) was one of three Leyland Leopard PSU3E/4Rs with Alexander T-type bodywork supplied in the summer of that year.

A rear three-quarter view of the same vehicle on Waverley Bridge. All three Leopards were later sold to Scarlet Band, Ferryhill, and all three subsequently entered preservation.

1979 saw a return to Duple bodywork but continued adherence to the Leyland Leopard, in this case the PSU3E/4R variant. Numerically the last of the three, 250 (NSX 250T) is here seen taking on passengers for a city tour on Waverly Bridge a few weeks after it was delivered.

Severe delays in the bodying of new Seddon Pennine VIIs in 1977 led Eastern Scottish to hire ten of Lothian's withdrawn PD2As, rendered surplus by delivery of Atlanteans and by OMO conversions. Between 20 June and 2 July, they were used in relation to the Royal Highland Show at Ingleston. YWS 601, 602 and 617 await their turn at Eastern Scottish's St Andrew Square bus station.

607 (YWS 607) turns out of St Andrew Square bus station en route to Ingleston in summer 1977. A Scottish Omnibuses uniformed employee stands on the kerb contemplating the unusual sight of a madder and white vehicle emerging from the SBG stronghold.

The vehicle displays the must-have fashion accessory of new double-deckers in the early 1960s, an illuminated offside advertising panel. This feature was dropped from subsequent orders.

In addition to the hire of PD2A/30s, Eastern Scottish also hired some PD3/6s. The initial batch, 656/58/59/63/65/71, arrived in mid-July 1977 and there were some reported problems in manoeuvring these 30-foot buses in St Andrew Square bus station, leading to five being returned to LRT. These difficulties cannot have been insuperable as the rest were retained for a short time and even supplemented by two others, including 662 (ASC 662B), seen here at the uppermost stance at St Andrew Square bus station with labels announcing its intended destination of Balerno by way of Slateford. Several of the PD2As were also pressed into duty on services 52 and 53 to and from Balerno to the west of the city.

Eastern Scottish continued to have difficulties in delivery of new vehicles, and, as a result, in July 1977 purchased 601–03/06–08/10–13/17/38 from Lothian, and took some further examples in the August. YWS 638 causes confusion to a dog-walker as it passes through Balerno in Lothian livery, with an Edinburgh Corporation crest on the front grille, though in fact it was on Scottish Omnibuses' books as HH312.

Former Lothian Region Transport 612 (YWS 612), freshly outshopped as Scottish Omnibuses' HH309, drives though Musselburgh in its early days with its new owner.

Newly repainted YWS 611, now HH308, heads towards Musselburgh through Cockenzie in the summer of 1977. At the time this was definitely Eastern Scottish territory, where the Edinburgh municipal buses dared not tread, but nowadays it is served by Lothian Buses.

In the background is a covered conveyer associated with the power station at Cockenzie, then new but now decommissioned.

While Scottish Omnibuses was borrowing rear-platform vehicles to supplement its services, Lothian Region Transport was in the position of being able to retire its last examples of the type. 610 (YWS 610) was secured for a final tour of the city by a group of enthusiasts and is seen here at The Shore, Leith, during a photographic stop during which several of the company contemplate the still depths of the Water of Leith.

Purchasers of used Edinburgh buses were usually independents but in 1975, following the loan of PD2/20 600 (LWS 600), fourteen similar buses were purchased by Dundee Corporation and its successor Tayside Regional Transport. These buses were prepared for their new owners at Shrubhill, and it is there that former Edinburgh 526 (LWS 526), Tayside 9, stands awaiting delivery.

These buses seemed to have been good value to their new owners. OFS 761, former Edinburgh Corporation 761 and here still in Dundee Corporation green, became a trainer with Tayside and is seen in the company of an Alexander (Midland) Bristol Lodekka trainer on the left and one of Dundee's ill-starred Alexander bodied Fleetline saloons, T4, on the right.

The Tayside traffic was not one-way. 10 October 1976 saw a short period where Tayside Ailsa 113 (NSL 113R), on loan to Ailsa Trucks as a demonstrator, was used in Edinburgh on service 23. Here it heads down Trinity Road towards the Lennox Row terminus, bearing rather contrasting stickers carrying the Lothian Region Transport legal lettering.

The introduction of driver-only operated services spelled the end for the Orions, but a good few were sold for further service. An early departure from the fleet was 405 (LFS 405), acquired by Gibson of Moffat in 1971, photographed here in the centre of the town.

439 (LFS 439) was also withdrawn in 1971 and passed to Palmer of Douglas and later to Wilson, Carnwath, in whose yard I found it – looking very smart – in 1975.

As well as the PD2/20s that the municipal operator retained as trainers, two others were acquired for a similar role by the South of Scotland Road Transport Training Centre, Straiton, Loanhead. 756/57 (NSF 756/57) were acquired in March 1975. Here, NSF 756 drives along a remarkably quiet Princes Street.

Alexander-bodied Titan PD3/6 670 (ASC 670B) was new in 1964 and, together with similar 687 and 688, was sold in the summer of 1977 to Wilson of Carnwath, who adapted it to their livery by extending the area of white above the lower deck windows. It is seen here on their premises in 1978.

Withdrawn by Lothian in November 1976, 696 (ASC 696B), another example of the 1964 batch of Alexander-bodied PD3/6s, was quickly snapped up by A&C McLennen, Spittalfield, and is seen at their yard in 1979 looking very smart in their blue and white livery, with silver for the roof.

Alexander-bodied 1966 Leyland Titan PD3A/2 844 (EWS 844D) passed via the dealership of Booth, Rotherham to Moffat and Wiliamson, Gauldry in the summer of 1979. It was by then no stranger to foreign climes as prior to its withdrawal in early 1979 it had spent some time in Warrington to relieve a vehicle shortage there, returning home in November 1978.

Not every ex-Edinburgh bus that was sold for further service deserted the city forever. Former 667 (ASC 667B), a 1964 Leyland Titan PD3/6 with Alexander body, was purchased by Moffat, Cardenden, in 1977, but by the next summer was in the hands of Curran, Leith, and painted in a distinctive livery to promote Radio Forth. I photographed it outside Curran's premises on the corner of Graham Street and Newhaven Road in the winter of 1978.

From 3 May 1976, Leyland Titan PD2A/30 648 (YWS 648) was one of a number of Edinburgh vehicles on loan to Tyne & Wear PTE, who had been experiencing a vehicle shortage. It still carried the number blind that the PTE had fitted when it was acquired by the Craigmillar Festival Society in late 1976.

A curiously similar sequence of events pursued Alexander-bodied Leyland Titan PD3A/2 EWS 837D, former 837. It, too, spent some time after withdrawal by Lothian on loan in the northern part of England, to Warrington Borough Council in this case. In August 1979 it was sold to the Craigmillar Festival Society, but the livery applied by the society was considerably less elaborate than on the PD2A.

Edinburgh retired its coaches at a relatively young age, in order to keep the fleet up to date. 1974 saw the withdrawal of Duple-bodied Bedford SB5 212 SC and its sale to St Augustine's school. In this 1975 photograph it is at Central garage, so presumably there was some arrangment whereby the Transport Department provided maintenance. In 1979 the coach passed to Tayside Police as a mobile control room.

Edinburgh had taken 100 Leyland Tiger Cub PSUC1/3 buses with Weymann bodies in 1959 and 1960. However, the removal of several low bridges allowed many of them to replaced by double-deckers in 1966 and the fifty vehicles of the SWS-registered batch were sold to Ulsterbus. By the late 1970s these had been withdrawn, and many found themselves neglected and abandoned in various locations in the six counties. Here, former Edinburgh Corporation 40 (SWS 40), ex-Ulsterbus 1040, quietly decomposes in Dromore, County Down, Northern Ireland, with its Edinburgh Corporation badge still in place on the front.

Perhaps because Edinburgh replaced its coaches after a fairly short service life, many went on to see further service elsewhere. A typical example was 230 (PSC 230G), which was new in 1969, but which by 1976 had passed to the Lincolnshire operator Appleby of Conisholme. It is photographed here in Grimsby in 1979.

389 (SSF 389H) had a prolonged existence, as it ended up with Northern Ireland Water as their Waterbus, in which form it persisted until disposal in 2007. (Courtesy of Paul Green)

Starting from its days as a cable tram depot, Shrubhill works had provided engineering support for the Transport Department. In this 1976 view, a PDR1/1 , a PDR1A/1 and an AN68 receive attention.

One unusual exhibit at an open day at Shrubhill works in 1974 was 342 (PSC 342G) on the tilt table. The plaque informs the reader that double-deckers have to tilt unsupported to an angle of 28 degrees with a simulated full passenger load on the top deck, together with driver and conductor (even though this was a driver-only operated vehicle). The 28 degree stipulation remains to this day, though an allowance for the conductor has been deemed redundant.

An essential tool of any large bus operator in the 1970s was a recovery vehicle. Edinburgh had a smartly liveried Leyland for the purpose registered on trade plates, as was the usual way of things in those days. 153S has in charge a PD2 that has disgraced itself and, judging by the queue of traffic behind, is making slow progress.

An Edinburgh bus facility no longer used for that purpose is Leith garage. This 1975 image shows a variety of PDR1/1 and PDR1A/1 Atlanteans and a PD2A/30, all with Alexander bodywork. Leith became Edinburgh's first garage providing solely driver-only operated services when service 16 was converted on 4 July 1976, but closed as a bus garage only a few months later in early 1977. After the building's closure as a bus garage it was used to accommodate other council-owned vehicles. Its services were transferred to Central and Marine.

This photograph at Central garage in the early days of driver-only operation finds Leyland Atlanteans PDR1A/1 307 (PSC 307G) and PDR1/1 863 (JSC 863E) awaiting their next turn of duty. Both buses have Alexander bodies. 863 later found employment with Scarlet Band, County Durham.

ASC 655B, a Leyland Titand PD3/6 of 1964 vintage, was the victim of an accident on Wednesday 18 June 1975 when a lorry struck the bus as it was turning right into Oxgangs Avenue. The impact caused the bus to topple over resulting in injuries to nine on board. Much of the damage seen here, however, was caused by the efforts of the crane to right the vehicle after the accident. It is seen outside Shrubhill works prior to scrapping.

Weymann-bodied Leyland Tiger Cub PSUC1/3 77 (VSC 77) sustained significant accident damage in 1974, resulting in its withdrawl. The battered remains are seen here at the corporation's Shrubhill works.

Accident-damaged PD2A/30 627 (YWS 627) was withdrawn in March 1976. Here it awaits disposal at Marine garage. The prize money advertised by Vernon's Pools seems modest by today's National Lottery standards!

By 1974, withdrawals of Edinburgh's then-iconic MCW Orion-bodied Leyland Titan PD2s were continuing in earnest. Some went for further service, but many for scrap. Bernard Hunter at Gilmerton received a good few, as seen here in the company of a Tiger Cub, all in various stages of dismemberment.

During 1974 the training fleet was expanded to fifteen vehicles, all Titan PD2/20s. A new livery for the trainers was introduced at about that time, and in 1976 the training fleet was renumbered from T1-15 to TB1-15. This shot at Marine garage captures three of the trainers among Alexander-bodied Titans. OFS 776 is still numbered T8, OFS 800 only bears the number '15' while awaiting the replacement of the 'T' with 'TB', and OFS 796 proudly shows its shiny TB fleet number – though it is reported that it never actually operated after renumbering.

Not an Edinburgh bus, but a bus in Edinburgh and very much of an Edinburgh style. At the Scottish Commercial Motor Show in November 1975, Leyland exhibited what it asserted was the thousandth Atlantean delivered to the Glasgow municipal fleet. The show bus, KSU 863P, bearing the fleet number LA1000, was subsequently despatched on a tour to wave the flag, so to speak, or at least the fetching rosette visible in the top deck front window. Hence the unusual appearance of a Glasgow municipal bus at Edinburgh's Marine garage. Apart from the livery it looked hardly out of place at all, as the style of Alexander body was somewhat influenced by Ronald Cox, general manager of Edinburgh Corporation Transport until his appointment in 1973 as director general of Greater Glasgow PTE.

Despite the fleet number asserting the contrary, this bus was not actually LA1000 – that honour fell to KSU 876P and 863 was later renumbered LA987.

TB6 (NSF 771) heads south along Leith Walk in 1978. Originally 771, this MCW-bodied Leyland Titan PD2/20 was one of the first to receive the revised trainer livery seen here in summer 1974.

A view of a training bus familiar to car drivers in Edinburgh in the 1970s. T15 (OFS 800) carries both a warning to the motorist and an invitation to prospective Transport Department employees.

Edinburgh's buses have always been well presented. At Central garage, Leyland Atlantean PDR1A/1 355 (SSF 355H), with Alexander bodywork, receives the attentions of a hose after a hard day's work.

Still to be found near Hibernian Football Club's Easter Road ground in 1976 was this archaic bus stop flag from a much earlier era.

Edinburgh's first foray into more prominent advertising on buses fell to the PD3s. 673 (ASC 673B) acquired a largely yellow scheme promoting Cutty Sark whisky, its appearance being described by one observer as 'hair-raising'. Among others, schemes followed for Croall's garage and, as seen here on 663 (ASC 663B), M&W Personnel.

On 25 March 1976, 36 (BFS 36L), an Alexander-bodied Leyland Atlantean AN68 based at Leith Garage, introduced the Edinburgh populace to the all-over advertising bus with this scheme for Carlsberg. This development had required permission from Lothian Region Council, who had earlier approved a maximum of eight all-over advertising buses. It is seen descending Leith Walk, approaching St Paul's church, Pilrig on one of its first forays in its new livery. It returned to fleet livery in April 1977.

Another early recipient of an all-over advertisement was 37 (BFS 37L), a 1972 Leyland Atlantean AN68 with Alexander body. For about two years from May of 1976, it extolled the virtues of the Barclaycard. It is pursued along York Place by one of Scottish Ominbus' Bristol Lodekkas.

Possibly the most startling of the early all-over advertisment liveries used by Edinburgh was this treatment for the Edinburgh wax museum. One of the short-window Atlanteans, 817 (EWS 817D) was selected for this as it suited the design of the advertisement better than the panoramic-window alternatives. Here, 817 ascends The Mound in summer 1976.

939 was one of the vehicles chosen to be painted in a silver livery to commemorate the Queen's Silver Jubilee in 1977. Here it is in Princes Street in that year advertising Bell's whisky, though it is not clear if Her Majesty herself enjoyed the beverage. 939 benefitted from this eyecatching livery until August 1979.

One of the more unusual vehicles to operate for Edinburgh Corporation Transport in 1972 was the Crompton Leyland Electricars Limited CAX379K. This Willowbrook-bodied vehicle (B9F plus seventeen standee) was constructed on a modified British Leyland 900FG chassis, and had a range of 35 miles in city traffic, with a maximum speed of 25 miles per hour.

Still in use some twenty-two years after delivery was former Edinburgh Corporation Transport 810 (HWS 775), a Leyland Royal Tiger PSU1/17 that was orignally fitted with a Leyland B40R body, with an open rear platform of the style usually found on front-engined saloons. The corporation later converted this bus and the other members of its batch to front-entrance coaches in the style seen here. After withdrawls, several found new homes with the social service department, Greenlea Old People's Home, or, as seen here in 1974, with the Leonard Cheshire Home on East Trinity Road. The chassis of this vehicle is in store with the Scottish Vintage Bus Museum.

At the very beginning of the 1970s, the training fleet consisted of two Guy Arab III/MCCW saloons of 1948 vintage, ESG 652 and ESG 653. The former, latterly numbered 839 but previously 739, is seen here in Central garage at the very end of its career in 1970. The two Arab III saloons were replaced as trainers by two Arab IV deckers, NSF 901 and NSF 903. ESG 652 was subsequently preserved and remains with us to this day.

In contrast to the above, and in the same location five years later, the newly restored 739 looks resplendent once again.

Possibly the oldest Edinburgh bus to be found in the 1970s was this pre-war former Edinburgh Corporation Transport Daimler COG5 with Metro-Cammell body. Former WS6372, numbered G12. It inhabited a field near Biggar till 1976, when it was broken up.

Edinburgh Corporation Transport 135 (FSC 182), a Daimler CVG6/MCCW built to a design favoured by Birmingham, had been withdrawn at the end of the 1960s but in the seventies was a regular attendee at preserved vehice events, such as the 1975 Dunbar Rally. This magnificent machine remains in preservation to this day.

This elegant vehicle with its detailed grille and fine lining out is former Edinburgh Corporation 314 (JWS 594), which is taking part in the vehicle parade accompanying the 1978 Greater Glasgow PTE open day. This Guy Arab II was new to the London Passenger Transport Board in 1943 with a Park Royal utility body. It was purchased as one of a number of ex-London buses by Edinburgh in 1952 and rebodied by Duple Nudd. During its Edinburgh career it was fitted with a Gardner 6LW engine to replace the original 5-pot unit; the modification meant it acquired a slightly longer bonnet, and in common with the other buses of that batch it also gained the then-standard Edinburgh BMMO-style slatted grille. Following withdrawal it was acquired for preservation and subsequently re-engined with a 5LW. A replica front was fitted to reproduce the buses' appearance when first in service in Edinburgh.

This preserved Edinburgh and District horsebus was taken out of retirement in 1979 for an open day at Lothian Region Transport's marine garage. The two fine chestnuts took visitors on a short trip round the site. For most of the 1970s the bus had been an exhibit at Edinburgh's little-publicised Transport Museum at Shrubhill, where it had for company, amongst other exhibits, a steam roller and preserved tram 35.